CW00864392

Journey of a Seer

Journey of a Seer

Ian Ormesher

2017

Copyright © 2017 by Ian Ormesher

All rights reserved. This book or any portion thereof may not be reproduced or used in any manner whatsoever without the express written permission of the publisher except for the use of brief quotations in a book review or scholarly journal. Unless otherwise identified, Scripture quotations are taken from the HOLY BIBLE, NEW INTERNATIONAL VERSION®, Copyright © 1973, 1978, 1984 International Bible Society. Used by permission of Zondervan. All rights reserved.

Cover photograph "The Tired Motorcycle" by The Roving Doctor. Used with permission. Artwork by Anna Goodman.

First Printing: 2017

ISBN 978-0-244-90271-1

Dedication

To Ross Paterson.

You invested in me as a young man of God. You taught me so much, in word and deed; planted seeds that are still bearing fruit; first introduced me to China and let me pour water on your hands.

Thank you. I am eternally grateful

Contents

Endorsements

Ian is the real deal! I've had the privilege of mentoring him for a while and can attest to his delight in God as well as his hunger to know Him better. His ability to ask questions and push until he gets every detail out of you certainly keeps you on your toes, needing to have an explanation ready! I've enjoyed watching him change and grow as he put into practice all that he has learned and I know there's still more to come. The things you read in this book may surprise you but there is always more of God for us to experience and enjoy. Come ready to be stretched and encouraged to move more in the prophetic yourself so that many people will be helped to know the love of God and His purpose for His church in the nations. I trust you will enjoy this book and you will continue to make His name famous where you are.

- **Angela Kemm**, Prophetic Evangelist. City Church Cambridge & RM Prophetic Team

Ian helpfully takes us with him as he unpacks how he discovered the realm of the seer. This book is full of seer experiences but deeply rooted in biblical truth. It will help you walk out your own journey with God irrespective of how prophetic you think you might be. Rich in examples and helpful pointers, Ian will bless and help you discover how to be a seer for yourself!

- **Julian Adams**

Ian has written a helpful and fascinating guide to the realm of 'seeing in the spirit'. Using his own journey as a provocation, Ian invites all of us to seek Jesus for a clearer hearing of His words. I encourage you to read this book, learn from Ian's wisdom and put it into practice wherever God has placed you.

- **Phil Wilthew**, author of Developing Prophetic Culture

Acknowledgements

First I would like to say thank you to Jesus, who took all my sin on the cross and gave me new life.

I'd also like to thank my wife, Mandy. She's a truly amazing woman. She's followed me round the world on some crazy adventures. She's always loved me. We're so different – like chalk and cheese – but what's great about that is my weaknesses are her strengths and visa-versa. I get to live my life twice, because I live it not just through my own eyes, but hers as well.

I'd like to thank Angela Kemm, whom God brought into my life when I was so bored and turned it upside down. She's still doing that!

I'd like to thank Anna Goodman, who continues to challenge and inspire me. This book has happened mainly through her encouragement. I've enjoyed watching her grow in the prophetic and am excited about all that God has in store for her.

Introduction

It's always good to have goals when writing a book. I have two reasons for writing this particular one. The first came when I went through a "fire tunnel" at Kings Arms Church in Bedford. A person laid hands on me and said, "You will write a book that I will want to read". I believe this is that book. The second is that I feel God wants me to share my story to help others who've struggled with the things I'll share about. Some of the experiences I've had are super weird and people don't really talk about them. It took me a long time to figure out what they were for and how I could use them for ministry and to glorify God. Paul talks in 2 Corinthians about some of the heavenly experiences he had. When he begins talking about them, he tries to keep people from knowing they were his own experiences. He wanted to stay humble. In the time that he wrote, those sort of experiences were normal and people were accepting of them. These days it's the other way round. My hope in sharing my stories, is not that you'll think anything of me, but rather that you'll fall in love with Jesus and the Father more and more. God loves to communicate with us, to share His heart with us, to express His love to us. My prayer for you as you read this book is the same prayer Paul prayed for the Christians in Ephesus (Eph. 3:16-19). I pray that out of the Father's glorious riches He may strengthen you with power through His Spirit in your inner being, so that Christ may dwell in your hearts through faith. And I pray that you, being rooted and established in love, may have power to grasp how wide and long and high and deep is the love of Christ and to know this love that surpasses knowledge-that you may be filled to the measure of all the fullness of God.

Chapter 1: Early Life

My parents were Mormons. My Dad was an elder in the Mormon church. The Mormons have their own book called 'The Book of Mormon' which they claim is of the same standing as the Bible. As my Dad studied this book, he grew more and more uncomfortable with what it said and with the Mormon teaching. He didn't feel it was the same as the Bible and that they differed in some big ways. The final straw for him was that they taught that only black people were born with original sin. This was the "mark of Cain". My Dad, quite rightly, felt this was simply racist and he left the Mormon church. I was just seven at the time. However, he didn't just turn his back on the Mormon faith, he turned his back on all faiths.

So I grew up with a sense of God and a love for Jesus, but not really knowing where to find either of them. When I entered my teenage years I went on a search for God. I got into the occult and then into something called Kabbalah. Kabbalah is a Jewish form of magic that is based on the Bible. I believed that the power that Jesus used was the power of Kabbalah, because he too was Jewish. I would use it to cast spells and they would work. I became very aware of the power of the occult and used it for my own ends. But as anyone who has been involved in the occult will tell you, you start with feeling you can control these powers, but eventually they end up controlling you. I started having terrifying nightmares, where I'd wake up screaming. I heard and saw things moving in my room when I went to bed. I'd go to sleep with my covers wrapped around my head, so I couldn't hear or see those things. Often I would dream I was being literally dragged down to hell. When that happened I would start repeating the Lord's Prayer as it was the only thing I thought could save me. I'd wake up, turn my light on and open my Bible at Psalm 27 and put it down in the middle of my

Journey of a Seer

room. Why Psalm 27? Because when I randomly opened the Bible in the middle, it was the first passage I found that mentioned light. I desperately wanted light, but all I was finding was darkness.

I left school and went to University. I shared student accommodation with two other guys. One day someone knocked at my door and asked if I'd be willing to do a questionnaire. I could see she was a fellow student, so I said yes because I thought I'd be helping her out with some course assignment. She started by asking me questions about God – whether I believed in Him, what I believed about Him. Did I believe in Jesus? What did I believe about Him? I had this sophisticated philosophy worked out that fitted in with Kabbalah. However, the girl was a German exchange student and since English wasn't her first language I couldn't explain it to her. This made me think for the first time about what I really believed about these things. When she talked about God, Jesus and prayer, I could tell she had a real relationship with Jesus. That when she prayed, she was really talking to Him. This was the first real Christian I had ever met and I was blown away. At the end of our time together I said I would think about the things she had said, but I was not planning on giving it much more thought.

For the next three weeks, everywhere I went I kept bumping into her. I'd never seen her before and now I was seeing her all the time! Each time she saw me, she'd asked me if I'd thought about what we'd talked about. If I'd thought about Jesus. I realised that I did believe in God, that I did believe that Jesus was also God, so I had to make a decision about Christianity and about becoming a Christian. I couldn't say no, so I had to say yes! I knew that if I was going to give my life to Jesus, it could only be 100%. So on Sunday, March 28th 1982, at 11:00 AM I gave my life to Jesus. I confessed my sins, received His forgiveness through the Cross. I gave Him my old life and He gave me a brand new life in Him. Thank you Jesus!

4

When I told my friends I had become a Christian, they didn't want to know me anymore. When I told my family, they all laughed at me! They thought it was just a fad and that I would soon give it all up and find another faith to follow. The girl who had led me to the Lord had to return to Germany. I'd only been a Christian a few weeks. She told me to read the Bible - that it was true and I could believe it. She said that now that Jesus was living inside me He would guide me and lead me. She also told me that I needed to join a Church.

When I told my flatmates that I had become a Christian, one of them admitted that he was also a Christian! He told me later that he'd been so scared of me he hadn't told me before! He was Charismatic and told me about "speaking in tongues". I asked him if it was in the Bible and he showed me that it was. Then I asked if I could hear it. So he spoke in tongues and my heart went on fire! I knew this was from God. He gave me a book by Dennis Bennett called "9 O'Clock in the Morning" that was about the gifts of the Spirit. It had a checklist of things to confess/repent of if you'd been involved in them in the past. They were all things to do with the occult. I pretty much ticked every box in that list! So I prayed the prayer of confession that was in the book and received forgiveness for those things, in faith, based on 1 John 1:9 "If we confess our sins, He is faithful and just to forgive our sins and cleanse us from all righteousness". It felt like I had just had a shower and was now incredibly clean. My flatmate then invited me along to a Full Gospel Business Men's Fellowship International (FGBMFI) meeting. Whilst I was there, people laid hands on me and I was baptised in the Holy Spirit. Then I, too, started speaking in tongues. I'd only been a Christian a few weeks, so I thought this was all very normal.

Word got out to my classmates that I had become a Christian and one of them also owned up to being a Christian (and also being scared of me!). He invited me along to his Church, so I went with

Journey of a Seer

him. The Church was a Brethren Church. On Sunday mornings they had a breaking of bread meeting. This consisted of people sitting in a circle, sharing things from the Bible, singing songs and then breaking bread together. It seemed to me to be a great opportunity to practice the gifts of the Spirit, which I'd read about in the Bible and seen at the FGBMFI meetings. One morning I stood up and gave a tongue, then sat down and waited for someone to give the interpretation. Most people seemed really embarrassed. I waited a bit, then stood up again and gave the interpretation, since no-one else seemed to be giving one. After the meeting one of the Elders of the Church took me aside and told me that they didn't believe in speaking in tongues. "But it's in the Bible", I said, "Why don't you believe in it? You DO believe the Bible is the word of God don't you?" He told me that I wasn't to speak in tongues anymore in one of their meetings. The following week I stood up and gave a prophecy. Again I was taken aside by an Elder and told that they didn't believe in prophecy either. In fact, they didn't believe in any of the gifts of the Spirit and I wasn't to bring any of them to their meetings. I was a bit taken aback. It didn't make sense. I knew the gifts of the Spirit were from God and I had seen the fruit of them in my life and others. They gave me a book called "Signs of the Apostles" published by "Banner of Truth". It claimed that all the gifts of the Spirit had disappeared with the Apostles and that now that we had the complete Bible we no longer needed them. Their viewpoint is called "Cessationism" since they believe the gifts of the Spirit have ceased to be available to the Church of today. So I studied the Bible more to see if what they believed was true. I couldn't find any support for their argument in Scripture. In fact, I found the opposite to be true. If you're interested in finding out more about this, I would highly recommend "Surprised by the Spirit of God" by Jack Deere. He was a cessationist who changed his view when he was surprised by the Spirit of God.

It turned out that there was a small group of secret Charismatics in the Church, led by a man called Stan Royden. Stan was a prophet and took me under his wing. I joined his house group and he introduced me to all things Charismatic. There was a big Charismatic revival going on in South Chard, Somerset. Stan would lend me their tapes and I was introduced to Ian Andrews and Harry Greenwood. I particularly liked Harry Greenwood, who also was prophetic. Stan mentored me and I grew in the prophetic under him. He taught me how to prophesy in the breaking of bread meeting without it appearing to be prophecy! He'd take me to monthly Charismatic meetings in Chester where I'd get "charged up", ready for the month ahead. I am so grateful for the time he invested in me at such an early point in my Christian life. Being a Charismatic in a non-Charismatic Church was an interesting time for me, however the Brethren taught me a love and respect for the Bible that I have never lost.

I tried out as many gifts of the Spirit as I could. But I was particularly drawn to prophecy. I found that when the Holy Spirit starting moving in power, all I wanted to do was prophesy! Some of the words I gave at the beginning would make me cringe now, I'm sure. I had a lot of zeal, but not a whole lot of love. But they were often accurate and God used them to speak into people's lives. I have learnt over time that it is really important to give words with love. I'm always striving to be more accurate with what I give. I'm also striving to be more loving. If you've given a word in love, it also makes it better if you fluff it and get it wrong. At the end of the encounter, accurate or not accurate, the person should always feel loved – by you and by God.

Speaking in tongues

Not long after I became I Christian I read a book by Jackie Pullinger called 'Chasing the Dragon'. Jackie had gone to Hong Kong to be a missionary and ended up working with drug addicts and seeing them become Christians. She had a radical strategy for getting people through the "Cold Turkey" of coming off drugs. She would get them to pray in tongues. And they would be able to come off drugs, without any major withdrawal symptoms. She really recommended speaking in tongues and she would do it at least 15 minutes a day. After she started doing this she saw major fruit in her ministry. 15 minutes sounded like a long time to just speak in tongues! But I decided to give it a go. I found it hard at first, but after a while it became second nature. I learnt how to do it quietly under my breath, so I could do it when I was on the bus, or on the train. I also read what Paul said in 1 Cor. 14 about praying with your mind and praying with your spirit. So I practised praying in tongues at the same time as praying prayers in English in my head. It was a bit like rubbing your stomach and tapping your head at the same time, but eventually it also became second nature. Now, when I go out to pray, I'll be praying in tongues and praying with my mind at the same time. There isn't usually anyone else around, so I don't need to do this quietly! If I'm out walking in the street, I'll put my coat collar up, so I can pray in tongues into my coat. If people see you walking down the street and muttering to yourself, it's not a good thing!

The Call

It was at this time that God called me to be a prophet. I was reading Isaiah 6 where Isaiah has a vision and sees the Lord. When I read the bit where the Lord says, "Who can I send", I felt the Lord asking me that question too. I answered, as Isaiah did, "Here am I Lord, send me".

Chapter 2: Call to Mission

Because someone from another country had come and told me about Jesus, I felt I also wanted to go to another country and tell people about Jesus. I felt there was a missionary call on my life. I started going along to Operation Mobilisation (OM) prayer meetings to pray for the nations and to pray for missionaries as they were being sent out. I asked which were the hardest nations to reach? People told me they were the Muslim countries. So I decided to take a year out from my course and go and work with Muslims in Germany with OM. Before I could do this, I needed to get approval from my eldership. Because my elders weren't Charismatic, I didn't feel they were spiritual enough to hear from God about my going to Germany with OM. But I laid my application before the Lord and said that if He wanted me to go, He would have to get the elders to agree, because I wanted to submit to their authority. So I gave them my application. After a few weeks they gave it me back. They refused to approve my application, as they said I was too immature to go. I was devastated and went back to the Lord. He said that it was more important that I submit to the leadership. That submission was the freedom from always having to be right. He also told me that when the time was right, He would lead me to an Antioch sending Church. He gave me Acts 13. So I put mission on the back burner and focused on the prophetic.

I began to notice that I was "seeing" things in the Spirit. I got involved in deliverance and would "see" the demons and cast them out. They would have names written on them, so I could address the spirit as I cast it out. I would see demons on top of buildings and their shape and size was significant to the building they were on. When I sat next to certain people I would get overwhelmed by feelings of lust, or anger, or some other thing. I realised that these weren't actually my feelings but rather the spirits that were affecting the person I was sitting next too. I would look into people's eyes and I could hear their hearts. Good and bad. I wouldn't just see demons, I would see angels too. I decided to chat with a friend of mine who had a lot of experience in the Charismatic. I told him about all of this and asked him how he handled these experiences and what they were for. I assumed all Christians experienced these things. He gave me a look like I was truly a weirdo and told me he had never had any of those experiences and didn't know what I should do with them. That's when I realised, for the first time, that these things were unusual. So I decided to keep them all to myself and not tell anyone else. I didn't tell anyone again about them for over 30 years. I never stopped having these experiences in the meantime. I just kept them to myself.

First Vision

I found it difficult to witness to my parents, particularly my Dad. He was very anti-religion and he had seen me at my worst. One day I was praying for my Dad and I had a vision. I was in heaven and I was looking down and I saw my Dad in Hell. He was surrounded by fire and was looking up at me. He said to me, "Why didn't you tell me?" After that vision I never had a problem talking to my Dad about my faith or Jesus!

Through a sequence of events I found myself on a leadership course in York. Two of the main people running this course were Alex Buchannan and Ross Paterson. Alex was a powerful prophet. I always found him to be a scary guy! I've never met anyone else who carried such a sense of holiness and the fear of the Lord. He was very much an Old Testament kind of prophet. He would prophesy over Christians their need to repent of certain things, with a warning that God would judge them if they didn't. And quite literally people would drop to the floor and die when they didn't change! He was the first prophet of such an anointing that I had ever met and I thought that was how all prophets were to act. But he was also a very loving man. He had such a heart for the poor. He and his wife were counsellors to many leaders and he had much wisdom from the Lord. He also loved reading the Bible. He would often ask in meetings who had read their Bible at least once. I was always shocked so few people would put their hands up. He had a goal to read the Bible as many times as his age. He achieved that goal and kept it up. But he didn't read it so he could boast about it. He did it because knowing the Bible is the best way to grow in the prophetic. You get to know the language that God uses when He speaks. Alex inspired me to read the Bible more than once and to get the Word of God inside me. I would encourage you to endeavour to read the Bible as much and as often as you can. I have found a rhythm over the years for reading the Bible in six months and reading it in a year. I did the six month rhythm before I had kids! There are Bibles you can get that cover the Bible in a year. Or you can follow a reading plan. But don't get put off by how long it takes you to read through the Bible. The important things is that you read all of it at least once in your life. There are words of love that God has inspired and put in His word for you, just waiting to be read. Before I read the Bible, I'll always pray and ask the Holy Spirit to speak to me through the passage I'm about to read. He inspired it, so He knows it best. He makes the words come alive and speak to my heart.

One day Alex gave me a significant, life-shaping word. He confirmed my call to the prophetic, but said that I wouldn't enter into my ministry until I was mature in age. In the meantime, God was going to give me an apprenticeship, where I would get to train in many different things. All of these would help me when I finally began my ministry. He told me that I would be a significant voice to my generation. He also told me that demons would see me and tremble.

I was in my early twenties and I thought "mature in age" must mean in about 10 years' time! Little did I know how long that would actually turn out to be. In fact, it turned out to be over 25 years. God gave Abraham a promise too that took over 25 years to be fulfilled. If you're still waiting on promises that God has given to you a long time ago, I want to encourage you to persevere in your waiting. Don't give up hope. Be like Abraham, who "against all hope, Abraham in hope believed." (Rom 4:18)

The Dragon and the silver soldier

It was about this time that I had another vision. I was sitting on the back of a huge dragon, with a sword in my hand. I was bouncing up and down in my saddle – as though I was travelling places and going somewhere. But the truth was the dragon was standing still. And then it was like I suddenly woke from a dream and realised that I was going nowhere and that I had a sword in my hand that could do some damage to the dragon. So I slid off the back of the dragon, cutting it with my sword as I went. This caused the dragon pain and it howled and turned towards me. The dragon was huge and towered over me, so I looked for higher ground. Nearby was a cliff at the same height as the dragon's head. I climbed up there in order to fight the dragon. I noticed that there were other people there too, also with swords and also looking to fight the dragon. I began to fight. I had my sword and shield and began lashing out at the dragon. The dragon breathed out fire at me and the heat was intense, but I continued to strike out at it. All the clothes that I was wearing began to burn up in the heat. It seemed so futile to try and fight the dragon, but I continued to do it because it was obviously annoying it and making it angry. The heat and the light were so intense I could not see if I was hitting anything, but I continued to strike out. All my clothes and what appeared to be my flesh began to melt and drip down onto the floor. Then someone next to me began to strike out at the dragon with their sword. They managed to get a few good hits to the head and neck because the dragon was giving me all its attention. Then it roared and turned towards this other soldier and began to breathe fire on them. Now it was my turn to get some good hits at the dragon's head. Then it turned back to me again. Finally it turned away from me to another soldier on the cliff and I was left alone. I had become all silver. All my clothes and flesh had been burnt off me and this was all that remained. I looked dead and lifeless – like a toy silver soldier. Then a huge hand appeared, reached down and picked me up. Suddenly I came to life again, safe in His hand. But now I was a living silver soldier.

At the time I didn't understand this vision. Only years later would it finally make sense to me. So I'll come back to it later on in the book (there needs to be some reason for you to keep turning the pages!).

Chapter 3: First trip to Heaven

I had a vision in which I saw an angel standing in the sky. It looked like he was standing on a platform. He reached out a hand to me and said, "Come on up". I took hold of his hand and it felt like I was suddenly in a very fast lift going up into the sky. I found myself in heaven and there in front of me was Jesus and God the Father sitting on His throne. I immediately fell on my face and worshipped them. God told me to stand and He invited me to come and sit with Him on His throne. I sat down next to Him and He said to me, "Look" and gestured with His hand to look in front of Him. The whole Earth came into view and I could see peoples and nations. God shared things with me about His plans for the world; His heart for the lost; His love for His Son, Jesus and many other things. He shared some intimate parts of His heart with me and I was overwhelmed by the experience. When the vision finished, I was in a daze. I didn't want to move or change anything. I felt so full of His love and His Spirit. It was a precious time.

Deliverance

Over the years I've mentored a number of people. I've had varying success with this and have discovered a pattern. When someone has a strong desire to be mentored, then it always works. But if someone thinks it might be a good idea because someone else has recommended it, or they've been made to do it, then it doesn't work. If I end up having to chase the person, it always fails.

One evening I got a phone call from the wife of a person I was mentoring at the time – Joe (name changed for anonymity). She sounded very scared and told me that Joe had tried to do some deliverance and it had gone horribly wrong and could I please come round to their house and help. When I got to their house, Joe's wife answered the door. She looked terrified and told me they were upstairs. I told her it would be ok. I asked the Lord to send some big strong angels to help me and started walking up the stairs, praying in tongues. I could hear a commotion upstairs and as soon as I made my way upwards, things went ballistic! There was a lot of shouting and screaming. When I entered the room I could see Joe sitting in a corner of the room, looking really scared. And there, on the floor, was a mutual friend. He was twisting and writhing like a snake and he was speaking in a voice that wasn't his own. It was very deep and saying some awful things. I could see that the situation had got out of hand, so I bound the demon in the blood of Jesus and told him to be quiet. He immediately stopped talking and stopped writhing. I then went over to Joe and asked him what had happened. He said this demon had manifested in his friend and he had tried to cast it out, but it refused to go. It wouldn't listen to what he said. I assured him that it had to go if we told it to, in the name of Jesus. I could see he was scared, so I invited the Holy Spirit to come fill the room with His peace and power and laid my hands on Joe. He calmed down immediately. I then addressed the demon in the guy and cast it out in the name of Jesus. I could see it leave him, in the spirit. As is often the case, there were more than one demon in there, so I cast out each one as they came to the surface. I usually pray in tongues and command them to manifest, at the same time as looking to see if I can see any more demons. Sometimes I'll see them and they'll have their name written on them. Sometimes I'll ask them what their name is. But I don't like talking with demons, so I usually bind them in the blood of Jesus and command them to be quiet. Eventually he was free and we all thanked Jesus together.

The great thing about the whole experience was that it was "on-the-job" training. It was practical mentoring. I was able to teach him the importance of ministering from a place of peace. Also how we, as Christians, have authority over demons in the name of Jesus.

Call to China

As I previously mentioned, the other main person running the leadership course was Ross Paterson. Ross was an apostle. He took me under his wing and invested a lot of time in me. He would take me with him on prayer walks. I didn't know you could walk and pray at the same time before this! We would walk together, talk and pray. Ross planted "seeds" in me that even now I can see are bearing fruit. He loved God's word, he loved to pray and he also loved China. He was just starting a ministry called Chinese Church Support Ministries (CCSM) and was also involved in translating Derek Prince's teaching into Chinese and taking it into China. He was looking for people to stand with him in prayer, so I did just that.

Ross founded a Church in York called Acomb Christian Fellowship (ACF). His big message was Acts 13. He saw his Church as being an "Antioch sending Church". When I heard him talking about this, I remembered what the Lord had told me all those years before – that he would bring me to an "Antioch sending Church". That was when I knew I would end up in York and be a member of ACF and that they would send me out onto the mission field.

The more I prayed for Ross and his work, the more I prayed for China, the more I felt called to that land. But China is a huge place, with lots of different peoples. It's the most populous nation in the world. So I started asking God the question, "Where in China and when to go?"

Eventually my wife, Mandy, and I moved to York and joined ACF. In Easter 1995 I went to serve at Spring Harvest in their mission section, representing CCSM. They gave me an evening off and I was able to go to hear the main preach. Gerald Coates was preaching and at the end of the meeting invited people to come up to the front who "wanted to be a catalyst". I'm always up for those sort of things, so I went to the front, waiting for prayer. As I was waiting I started to see a vision. It was like watching a film, with a running commentary at the same time. I saw these very high, snow-capped mountains and it was like I was flying up above them. I looked down and could see a flat valley surrounded by high mountains. God said, "This is Tibet and this is where I've called you to". I arrived in the valley and stood in the middle of it. The ground where I was standing began to sink down and become like a big round crater. It was like the inside of a crucible and it began to get hotter and hotter. All around me became orange in the searing heat. Suddenly this stopped and the hollow had been filled in with me inside. I had become a seed planted in the land. It was then that I noticed a hill that was also in the valley. On the top of the hill I could see a very tall cross. It was glowing. Then the vision ended.

I came away from the meeting wondering where Tibet was! I'd never heard of the place. I discovered that Tibet was actually in China. So I signed up for a prayer trip to Tibet, to see if I could find the place I'd seen in the vision and to confirm that we were indeed to go there. That summer I went to Lhasa, the capital of Tibet. When I arrived there I saw the hill I had seen in the vision. It was exactly as I'd seen it – surrounded by mountains and in a flat valley. It had a television mast on top of it, not a cross. But it was the same. When I came back from my trip I told Mandy we were finally going. We spent a year raising prayer and financial support and in the summer of 1996 we gave up our jobs, sold all our things and went to Hong Kong, with a view to going to Tibet the following year.

We lived and worked in Hong Kong during the handover year. It was quite emotional watching the British flag go down and the Hong Kong flag go up at midnight on 1st July, 1997.

Chapter 4: Tibet

In the summer of 1997 we moved to Lhasa, Tibet. The Tibetans are one of the great unreached people groups of the world. There are over 5 million of them who have never heard about Jesus. Did you know that 98% of missionary effort is spent evangelising nations that already have a national Church? The main religion of Tibet is a form of Buddhism called (surprisingly) Tibetan Buddhism. It's very occultic. And very dark. It didn't matter if you believed in spiritual warfare or not, from the moment you arrived, as a Christian, you were under attack. But I loved it! Tibetans are very open about their demons. They give them offerings to keep them happy, so they won't trouble them. Some of their idols in their temples are so scary they would cover them with scarves because they were giving people nightmares! The patron deity and protector of Lhasa is called Palden Lhamo. She is responsible for bringing sickness, so people give her offerings so they won't get sick.

One time I spent the night in a friend's house and slept in a room where the Tibetan maid used to sleep. In the middle of the night I woke up and felt something dripping on my face from above me. I went to wipe it away, but there was nothing on my face. Very strange. I started to drift off to sleep, then I felt the dripping again. Again I went to wipe it away and again there was nothing on my face. I closed my eyes again and this time I felt a hand on my throat, trying to strangle me! I was starting to choke and tried to grab hold of the hand to stop the choking. But there was nothing there. I immediately got out of bed, put the light on and started praying in tongues very loudly! The next day I shared this at our team meeting. It turns out that this is a very common experience for Tibetans to have, but not westerners. Not quite the sort of thing I was looking to pioneer!

Journey of a Seer

The first time I ever went into a temple and saw one of the demons, I felt stirred in my spirit and started praying in tongues against it. As I did this, I felt this giant foot come down on my head and start pressing down. It was so strong I started to bend down to the ground. As I did this I could see the foot of the statue. And there under the foot I could see the bodies of people who weren't Buddhist believers. That would be me! So I stopped praying in tongues against it and was able to stand up again. Since that time I've never prayed against a demon whilst I'm in their temple. The way to defeat these demons is to take away their power base. If Tibetans turn to Jesus, people won't worship the demons anymore and their temples and power will disappear.

I would usually go into a temple to try and befriend a monk, or because I was curious about the way the Tibetans' worshipped their gods. Some of them were noticeably spiritually darker than others. I also had a friend who used to be a monk at Sera monastery and he would show me round and introduce me to his friends.

We lived on a compound, with three other flats. Some Tibetan monks moved into the flat next to ours and they would do their chanting at night. It seemed very loud and I couldn't work out why. Then when I was coming home one night I saw that they had a Karaoke machine and were chanting into the microphone. They'd pointed the machine at our wall! I was very tempted when I got home to put on some loud Christian music and point the speakers at their wall! When I shared this with my team leader, he said I should make sure that every day I put on my armour and pray warfare prayers against them. As soon as I started doing this, things went very quiet. It turned out their Karaoke machine broke and they could only chant quietly in their room. Warfare prayer works! Since then I've put my armour on every day. It's listed in Ephesians 6. I have some scriptures that I declare for each of the pieces and as I'm declaring them I picture myself putting it on. For example, I put on my shoes, which is the readiness of the gospel of peace. As I'm doing this I proclaim some scriptures that talk about peace. And I've made them personal. I'll say, "I put on my shoes, which are the readiness of the gospel of peace. I have great peace because I love God's law and nothing can make me stumble". And so on. You might ask, "Why do you keep putting the armour on, when you never take it off?" I just do.

One night I woke up to see snakes whirling and writhing on my ceiling. I got up immediately and started to pray in tongues. They were falling from the ceiling and on to the floor. I called for angelic protection and eventually all the snakes disappeared. The next day I discovered that it had been a special festival day and the monks in the monastery had been performing a very dark ritual.

After this, every night we went to bed, before we went to sleep, we would ask God to set big, large, angels around us to protect us. And He did keep us protected.

One of the elders of our Church came out to see us in Lhasa with his wife. We forgot to warn them about the spiritual warfare they were entering into. They stayed in our flat and on the first night heard what sounded like a large animal on the veranda trying to get into their room. It was banging against the balcony door. Then it was inside their room and banging inside the room. The husband threw his shoe at where he thought the noise was coming from and turned the light on. There was nothing in the room! When he shared about this in the morning we laughed and apologised for not warning him about what can happen at night. We'd never heard of anyone using a shoe to scare off demons before! I can assure you that he and his wife prayed for protection before they went to bed each night. And they weren't troubled again.

Journey of a Seer

But it wasn't all darkness. I was also involved in the underground Tibetan Church. These were brand new believers – first generation! They needed to be discipled and mentored. I witnessed the first time the Holy Spirit fell on the Tibetan believers. The first time Tibetans spoke in tongues. Paul said he wanted to preach where Jesus hadn't been preached before and not to lay on another's foundation (Rom. 15:20). I was getting to do the same. It was a unique and special time. A privilege.

After we'd been in Tibet for a couple of years, we decided we wanted to start a family. Westerners can't have children in Lhasa, because of the altitude. The growing babies can't get enough oxygen through the placenta. And then once the baby is born, you can't bring them back up to altitude until their lungs have formed properly. So we decided we would leave for a couple of years, have children, then return. We put our things in storage in Lhasa and returned to York. What a simple plan, we thought. What could possibly go wrong?

Chapter 5: York-Kunming-Cambridge

When we got back we found our Church in a period of change. I was in a meeting one time and saw what looked like an umbrella over this man's head. I asked the Lord what it was and He said, "A spirit of Absalom". I had no idea what one of those was! So when I got back home I read up about the story of Absalom. He was one of David's sons. You can read about his story in 2 Samuel Chapter 15. What he would do is listen to people's complaints and say, "If only I was Judge in the land, I would see that you got justice". He stole the hearts of the people and put himself forward as king. In the next meeting I saw the same man, again with the umbrella over his head and coming out from it were lots of black cords. These were attached to different people in the congregation. These people had hooks in their hearts and every now and again he would pull the cords as he said something and people would cry out in hurt and anger. There were things that had happened in our Church whilst we were away that a number of people had taken offence at and this man appeared to be taking advantage of it, with a view to putting himself forward as a leader. I thought I needed to share this with my lead elder, John Wilson. But how to put it in terms that would not make me sound too weird?! I tried my best and shared with him. That's when I discovered about the things that had happened whilst we were away. I said I would stand in prayer for my leader and that's what I did. Not just on this one occasion, but all the time I attended that Church. Eventually the man with the Absalom spirit split our Church and formed a new one. But we stayed with John.

Knowing when to share something that a see has been a bit of a journey. I started with assuming that everything was just for me. That if God showed me something about someone else or a place or country - that would be for prayer. But I've also discovered that sometimes God is showing me those things because He wants me to share it with the person. If that's the case, trying to put it into a language that people can understand is tricky. So I always ask the Lord to help me. But even then, I've had some people give me looks like, "what are you on about?!" They're a great learning opportunity. Next time I'll try and be clearer.

After this, John employed an evangelist, who eventually became an elder together with John. One time John asked me to pray for him and the Church, but he couldn't tell me why. People have often done this to me over the years – asked me to pray for things without telling me why. When I start praying, the Lord will often show me exactly what it is that I am praying for and His answer, insight, etc. Sometimes He'll give me a prophetic word for them. He'll show me visions, or even speak to me in dreams.

This particular time He showed me a scene, like Abraham and Lot. John (who was Abraham) was on top of a mountain and so was this other elder (who was Lot). They were choosing which part of the land to have each. The other elder wanted the best portion of land. And I felt the Lord say that there were two different visions, which needed two different portions of the land and it was time to part ways.

I shared this with John and that's when he told me that he had been given an ultimatum by the other elder to leave the Church, because he wanted it to himself (the best part of the land). There was a whole Church meeting arranged for the middle of the week where John was supposed to hand the Church over. But he decided to stay and the other guy left, taking half the Church with him. Another split! Once again, we stayed with John.

Our first child was born in 2000 – Emily. Not long after she was born Mandy started going very yellow and feeling very sick and tired. She ended up in hospital and almost died. She'd picked up a form of hepatitis in Tibet. This slowed our baby plan down a bit! In 2002 our second child was born – Isaac. We now started making plans to return to Tibet. Then we had our third child in 2005 – Reuben. Finally, in the summer of 2006 we flew out as a family to Kunming, China. Kunming is at altitude and we thought this would be a good stepping stone for our return to Tibet.

Kunming

A couple of days before we left to go to Kunming, a prophet friend of mine, Trevor Adie, gave me a word. He said that within two years I would be back again and that this would be ok because I would have done all that God wanted me to do. There wasn't much I could do with the word at the time. So I put it on the back burner.

We sold everything, including our house and moved to Kunming. Because we were planning on being out long term, I decided to invest in learning mandarin for a year and Mandy home-schooled our children. However, in March 2007, I woke up in the middle of the night breathless and with pains in my chest. My left arm felt numb. This lasted for about 10 minutes and was quite scary. We had a doctor in our team and after checking me over he recommended I fly out to Bangkok, Thailand and have some tests done on my heart. I flew out on my own and had some tests. Then some more tests. Finally I had an angiogram, which revealed that four major arteries to my heart were significantly blocked. They offered to give me a bypass that evening! I asked if they could wait for my wife and kids to come first, to which they agreed. Once they arrived I had my bypass. It was the first time in my life I had ever faced death. I'd wondered before if my faith would stand up should I ever find myself in this situation. But I had a great peace and knew He was with me. I knew that if I died, I would get to be with Jesus. But if I lived, I knew He still had work for me to do. Saying goodbye to my wife and kids before going to the theatre was the hardest thing I've ever done. They were all so young. When I woke up in intensive care afterwards, I knew God still had work for me to do.

We came back to the UK that summer, to prove to everyone I was still alive. However, not long after returning to Kunming, I had pains again in my chest. I no longer had health insurance, since no-one would insure me now. So I flew back to the UK on my own. My doctor in York said I shouldn't fly again for a while, so we decided it was time for us all to come back to the UK and to lay down the call to Tibet. Our Church sent out someone to help Mandy pack up the house and come back to York with the kids.

That was when Trevor's word was a real encouragement. We knew that even though we had come home earlier than we'd thought, we had still done all that God wanted us to do.

I also realised that the vision I'd had all those years ago, about the dragon, was also fulfilled. China is often depicted as a dragon and I had been in two battles with it. The last one had almost killed me – and I seemed dead. But God picked me up and restored me. I was now a silver soldier.

Someone from our Church in York said that God had given them a picture as they had been praying for me. I was walking across this plain with my family. All of a sudden this big horrible demon appeared and spewed out water at us, in order to kill us. Then God made a bridge appear, with four strong arches, and we were able to cross over the plain and avoid the river. This person who saw this picture noticed there was something unusual about the appearance of the demon. They did a Google image search and found out who they were. It was called Palden Lhamo. She asked me if that name meant anything to me! It makes sense that the patron deity of the city of Lhasa and also the goddess of sickness would want to kill me. I am so grateful to God that He stepped in and saved my life by giving me four strong bypasses.

Cambridge

Because I'd given up my job and we'd sold everything, including our house, when we came back to York we didn't have anywhere to live or any work. A friend of mine who was working in Cambridge got me a short-term contract writing some computer software. Then the work got extended. Then extended again. In the end we decided that we should move as a family to Cambridge. So in the summer of 2008 we made the move down South. What a culture shock for us Northerners!

Angel of the Church

At the beginning of the book of Revelation Jesus gives seven messages to seven different Churches in Asia. But he actually addresses his messages "to the angel of the Church in ..." (Rev 2:1,8,12,18; 3:1,7,14). I personally believe that each Church has an angel assigned to it. Whenever I visit a Church I will always ask God to show me the angel of that Church. The angel is actually very revealing to how things are at the Church. When we ended up in Cambridge we joined City Church Cambridge. This was a New Frontiers Church. Since we had been in a New Frontiers Church in York this made sense and we felt God confirmed the place to us. I asked God to show me the angel of the Church. I saw a large angel at the front, standing tall, but with his head down. He was holding a massive sword in both hands and it was stuck in the floor in front of him. His wings were folded in. If it's possible, he looked very, very bored (it would take a few years before he changed, but I don't want to jump ahead of the story!) I asked the Lord why He'd call us to this Church, if this was how things were. But I knew He had, so we stayed. I started asking the Lord to wake us up as a Church, to not pass us by.

Chapter 6: You're a Seer

I was attending a prophetic course at Kings Arms Church in Bedford with my good friend, Tom Robson. Whilst I was in a meeting I saw Jesus appear on the stage. Then I saw a ladder appear above His head and angels start to come down the ladder and move amongst the people in the meeting. The presence of God was strong that night and a number of people were ministered to. On the way home I decided to tell Tom what I had seen. He said it sounded like a "Seer" anointing. I asked him what that was and he told me he'd been listening to some talks by Jonathan Welton about "The School of the Seers". He gave me a copy of the talks and it was like this big light came on! Jonathan talked about similar experiences to mine. I also bought his book, with the same title and devoured that. He talked about Gary Oates, so I bought his book, "Open My Eyes, Lord". Finally I had an understanding of the things I was experiencing. Because both Jonathan and Gary had started seeing when they went on a Randy Clark ministry trip, I decided I'd try and see Randy Clark if I could. I had no idea who he was. I didn't know he was into healing and impartation. He came to Bath to do a conference and I went along. The first meeting I went to someone laid hands on me and I found myself on the floor. The Spirit was so heavy on me I couldn't get up! I was literally pinned to the floor and ended up being there for a couple of hours. Whilst I was there I saw the Lord appear in front of me, standing looking over me. His presence was so strong, I knew that if I hadn't already been on the floor I would have fallen there straight away. Then He bent down to me, to say something in my ear. He said, "My word is power" and then He disappeared.

Randy Clark has got to be one of the humblest public ministers I've ever come across. Whenever I talk to people about him, they've never heard of him! But I know that's how he wants it. Randy introduced me to impartation – the laying on of hands. He also instilled a passion in me to pray for the sick. Just like Jesus did.

I devoured every book that had "Seer" in it's title! That's when I came across James Maloney. I bought his books and went along to a conference he was doing in Scarborough. I asked God to show me what he was showing James, so I could learn. On the first night as he was preaching, I saw a big, tall angel standing off to the side. I knew it was James' angel. He looked dark and I thought, "Oh no! James has a demonic angel!" But then I saw other angels around him and they weren't attacking him. Quite the opposite. Then I saw this angel fly over to James' side, ready to do ministry. And I realised that he appeared dark because his skin was dark. That night, because there weren't many people there, James decided to tell people what he was seeing and explain it. I'd listened to many of his talks, before and after, but I'd never heard him do this in such detail at any other time. It was my answer to prayer! He said he was seeing words appear above people's heads and he would just read out what he saw. Sometimes he would see snapshots of how someone got a sickness. Sometimes he would see the part of the body that was ill. I saw some amazing, miraculous, healings that weekend. Cancer, quite literally, disappearing before my eyes. James combines healing with "seeing". As I watched him minister I said, "Lord, I want to minister like that too!"

Julian Adams

A prophet-seer called Julian Adams came to minister at our Church. At the beginning of the meeting I could see a big flurry of activity in the spiritual realm. I saw some angels put up a big, white sheet at the back of the meeting. Then I saw another angel set up something that look like a projector and he pointed it at the wall. Then I saw two angels standing at the side. Each of them was holding up a sword and the swords had something written on them. I bent my head so I could read what they said. On the one sword I read the word "Courage" and on the other sword I saw the word "Faith". When Julian began to minister he called one person up and I saw the angel with the "Courage" sword move from the side and stand in front of the person. Then Julian said that he believed God wanted to give the man courage for the things that God was calling him to do. As he said this, I saw the angel tap the man on each shoulder, like he was knighting him. Julian continued to prophesy over him. I saw Julian looking over the man's head as he did this. That's when I noticed that the angel with the projector was playing what looked like a film against the back wall, onto the white sheet that the other angels had put up. Julian would prophesy about the things that he was seeing on that sheet.

Then Julian called up another man. I saw the second angel, with the "Faith" sword, come over and stand in front of him. Julian told this man that God wanted to increase his faith and to be bold in God and take risks. As he said this, I saw the second angel plunge his sword into the man's heart and the man began to shake. Julian also prophesied other things that he saw for that man, that were being projected against the back wall.

I got really excited about this. I had always thought, up until this point, that seeing was just for prayer or for deliverance. I never knew it could be used for the prophetic! As I watched Julian minister and how he interacted with the spiritual realm, I said to God, "I want to do that! Please use me like this!"

At another meeting I was playing in the worship band, so I was on stage and could see what Julian was seeing. I saw this thick, milky, substance slowly come down on the congregation. I was thinking, "What's this?!" Then Julian said that he could see that the presence of the Holy Spirit was thick amongst us. Now I understood what I was seeing - what it meant and how to interpret it to people.

Journey of a Seer

I knew Julian was a very busy man and there was no way he'd be able to mentor me. Plus, he didn't know me from Adam. But seeing him minister set a desire in me to be mentored by someone who could help with the prophetic and seeing. I shared this desire with my accountability buddy and good friend Andrew Fraser. Andrew said, "You must meet my mother-in-law. I'm sure she'd be able to help you in some way". So he arranged for me to chat with her one day when she was visiting his family. Her name was Angela Kemm. I spoke with her for about 10 minutes and she answered all my questions! I'd never met anyone before who I could be so honest with about the things I was seeing and what to do with them. She knew exactly what I was talking about and didn't treat me as strange or weird. She gave me much wise advice. I'm sure you'd like to know what those questions were and their answers - but I'm afraid I can't remember them exactly! I've asked her so many questions, I can't remember which ones were first. After I've seen her minister, I'll say things like "when you asked that person about ..., how did you know to ask that?" If she says "I just know" I'll always press her for a better answer than that! Never settle for "I just know".

Angela invited me to come along with her as she ministered. I was to be part of the ministry team afterwards, going out and prophesying over people. At the first meeting I was standing in the worship and I saw boxes falling onto the stage. They were all wrapped up like gifts. Then someone came to the front and said that they believed that God wanted to give gifts to some people there tonight. I got excited – because that was just what I'd seen. After the meeting I talked to Angela and told her about the boxes that I'd seen. She told me that next time I should ask God to show me what was inside the boxes. At the next meeting I saw the boxes fall down onto the stage again, but this time I could actually see what was inside the boxes. There were different things in each one. I saw a catapult inside one box. Then I turned round to look at the congregation and

I saw one lady with that same catapult on top of her head! And I noticed it was the same for all the other boxes. I could see the corresponding object over someone in the congregation. When it came to the ministry time, I went up to these different people and prophesied over them, using the objects as the starting point. I asked the Lord what the object represented for them and then prophesied with His answer. I've found that the same object can mean different things for different people. This means I always have to go back to God for the meanings.

The next meeting I again saw some objects on the stage and spotted where they were in the congregation. This time Mike Betts, who was leading the meeting, came over to me and asked if I had anything for anyone who was there. I said I had a few things, thinking it would be for the usual ministry time later. But he said he wanted to build people's faith tonight and could I give them from the front before he preached. I'd seen Julian do it, so I knew it should work in theory – I just needed to step out in faith! So I went to the front and prophesied over the different people who had objects over them. At the end of the meeting Mike thanked me for giving the words. That's when I told him I'd never done it before! He said he couldn't tell and he would use me more. After that Mike would often ask me up to give words from the front for people. Very quickly I stopped seeing the objects on the stage first and would just see them over people. And now I can be called to the front without seeing any objects before and God will show me as I'm standing there. That's a lot scarier! But God always comes through. He's good like that – because He's a God who loves to communicate with his children.

The prophetic never gets any easier. There's always a part of me that dies as I do it. It's always by faith. It doesn't matter how many times you've been accurate in the past, you still need to be accurate with the word you are currently speaking now. That's why our motive has always got to be love. We must love the person that we're ministering to. Our words should be an expression of God's love to them. That way, even if we get it wrong, they should still feel loved by God and encouraged. I'm an introvert by nature and would much rather sit in a corner of a room reading a book. But when I know He's wanting me to speak something for Him I'll step up and give it, whatever the cost. If I'm not prepared to pick up my cross and follow Him I can't call myself His disciple.

My favourite object story is when I saw an ice-cream cone over someone. I said that I saw them in an ice-cream van handing out ice-cream cones to children. As they handed out the ice-cream cones God filled them with delicious ice-cream. The ice-cream was so delicious that adults started queuing up for them too - it was ice-cream that was tasty not just for children but adults too. The man came up to me afterwards and said that he was involved in children's ministry and was in the process of buying an ice-cream van! He wanted to use it to go to estates to evangelise. He also wanted to expand his ministry to not just be for children, but also to include youth, adults and families. The words I'd spoken had been a great confirmation and encouragement from God for him.

My other favourite object story is when I was in a meeting and I saw an object over a person who was sitting at the back of the meeting. I didn't have my glasses on, so it looked like they had a seagull over their head. I asked the Lord what the seagull meant. God said it wasn't a seagull but a dove! The man was a man of peace and that was what the dove represented. So I put my glasses on and could clearly see that it was indeed a dove. Ever since then I always minister with my glasses on so I can see better. If someone can please explain to me why I need physical glasses to see spiritual things more clearly, I'd be very happy to hear the reason!

Chapter 7: What is a Seer?

The Bible differentiates between a prophet and a seer. 1 Chronicles 29:29 says "As for the events of King David's reign, from beginning to end, they are written in the records of Samuel the seer, the records of Nathan the prophet and the records of Gad the seer". There are nine people in the Bible who are given the title seer:

- Samuel (1 Chronicles 29:29)
- Gad (1 Chronicles 29:29)
- Zadok (2 Samuel 15:27)
- Heman (1 Chronicles 25:5)
- Iddo (2 Chronicles 9:29)
- Hanani (2 Chronicles 16:7)
- Asaph (2 Chronicles 29:30)
- Jeduthun (2 Chronicles 35:15)
- Amos (Amos 7:12)

Eventually seers were called prophets. 1 Samuel 9:9 says "(Formerly in Israel, if a man went to inquire of God, he would say, "Come, let us go to the seer," because the prophet of today used to be called a seer.)". This was a change in the title, but not in the function. Both the prophet and the seer are called to speak forth the words of God, but they function very differently. Because the same word eventually was used for both a prophet and a seer, by the time we come to the New Testament there is no longer any mention of "seer". But there is still the office of the prophet, which also includes the seer (see Ephesians 4:11).

Why the distinction? I believe it has to do with the way that a prophet receives his revelation from the Lord. A seer would typically receive it through a vision or pictures. Amos is a really good example of that. Amos 7:7-8 "This is what he showed me: The

Journey of a Seer

Lord was standing by a wall that had been built true to plumb, with a plumb line in his hand. And the Lord asked me, 'What do you see, Amos?'" Amos saw something, and then the Lord asked him what he saw. In Amos 8:1-2 God again shows him something and asks him what he saw. In contrast, a prophet would receive their revelation often verbally, where the words would "bubble up" from within. The Hebrew word for prophesy is "naba" [Strongs 5012] which means "bubble up".

The Unseen Realm

So we fix our eyes not on what is seen, but on what is unseen. For what is seen is temporary, but what is seen is eternal (2 Corinthians 4:18)

How can you fix your eyes on what you can't see?!! This is obviously not talking about the physical realm, but the spiritual realm. To see this realm we need to use spiritual sight, not physical sight.

There's a story in the Bible in 2 Kings 8-27 about the king of Aram who was at war with Israel. Every time he planned to attack Israel God would tell Elisha where they would be and he then warned the king of Israel to avoid that place. This frustrated the king of Aram. When he discovered what was happening he decided that he needed to take Elisha out of the picture. He sent horses and chariots to surround Elisha and capture him. When the servant of Elisha got up in the morning and saw all those horses and chariots he got scared. But Elisha told him not to be afraid because

"Those who are with us are more than those who are with them." And Elisha prayed, "O LORD, open his eyes so he may see." Then the LORD opened the servant's eyes, and he looked and saw the hills full of horses and chariots of fire all around Elisha (2 Kings 6:16-17)

Elisha was already able to see in the spiritual realm with spiritual sight, which is why he wasn't afraid. He asked God to open his servant's spiritual eyes, so he could also see into the spiritual realm. Then his servant was also able to see the horses and chariots of fire. It would seem that the ability to see in the spiritual realm is a gift that can be given from God.

Another example of God opening someone's spiritual eyes so they can see in the spiritual realm is Balaam and his donkey (Numbers 22:21-35). So he doesn't get killed by the angel of the LORD for pursuing a reckless road, God opens his eyes so he can see what is really going on:

Then the LORD opened Balaam's eyes, and he saw the angel of the LORD standing in the road with his sword drawn. So he bowed low and fell facedown (Numbers 22:31)

Discerning of Spirits

1 Corinthians 12:8-10 lists the gifts of the Spirit. One of those gifts is discerning of spirits. People usually teach about this being the ability to discern the source of spiritual things – whether the source is the Holy Spirit, the human spirit or a demonic spirit. I believe it also means the discerning of spirits that are in the spiritual realm. It's a part of the seer gifting.

Chapter 8: Personal Angels

I believe that we have personal angels that God assigns to us. Acts 12:15 talks about this with Peter's angel. And Jesus said that the angels of children get to see the face of God. Sometimes God shows me people's angels.

Heidi Baker

Heidi came to Cambridge a few years ago. She has friends here. I went to hear her speak, as I had never seen her before. Before the meeting started she was on her knees praying. I saw a lot of angels standing around her. There must have been over 100 of them. They were like a huge wall and they were all linked together, arm in arm. They were all fiery angels and it looked like there was a huge wall of fire surrounding her. Then I saw her crying out to God and God sent down what looked like a powerful waterfall of water and a pillar of fire at the same time. I couldn't work out how fire and water could both be coming upon her at the same time – but they were! She was so thirsty for the presence of God and in need of the fire of God, to burn with passion within her. It was awesome to watch. I've never seen anyone else, before or since, with so many angels around them.

Andrew White

Andrew White was the vicar of Bagdad. He came to speak at Kings Arms Church one time. At the beginning of the meeting, while we were in worship, I saw angels standing in a circle just above the people in the main hall. They were all holding up flags and waving them. These flags were coloured blood red and in the centre of each one was a picture of a lamb that was slain. As they were waving them I could see blood dripping from each one. Standing behind these angels and also in a circle, were some massive angels. I've never seen ones so big! One of them was called Justice. Another Righteousness. One called Peace. One called Joy. I couldn't see the names of the others. They were standing very tall and shouting out to the Principalities and Powers, "Come and see! Come and see! Come and see the real thing. Come and see a son of the King who does not love his life unto death. Come and hear his testimony!" Then I saw the blood-red flags turn into a red carpet that came down to the feet of Andrew. A red carpet, fit for a son of the King.

My Angel

I know that I too have an angel who goes with me wherever I go. He walks behind me. Sometimes when I'm out praying in the dark in the early hours of the morning, I'll see my shadow in front of me, when there is no moon or light. It's usually when I'm praying hard for something. That seems to fire him up and I'll see this brilliance around me.

One time I was out praying in the fields behind my house. I was saying to God how I wished I had a big large angel like the ones I'd seen with other people. It was a quiet sunny afternoon and I was walking through a wheat field. It was perfectly still, with no wind. Just as I was saying these things I felt a big push in the middle of my back from behind. I turned round to see who had pushed me and there was no-one there! I saw the tops of the stalks of wheat immediately behind me moving, but the rest of the field was perfectly still. I asked God, "What was that?!" He said, "That was your angel! Stop complaining!"

Chapter 9: Visions of Heaven

I have often had visions of heaven. Sometimes God will call me up to heaven and I will sit with Him on His throne. He will share His heart with me, or show me the Earth and His plans for it. Quite often He will wake me in the middle of the night and tell me that He wants me to come up. When He does that I'll go downstairs, get some bread and wine, then take communion with Him. Then He'll take me up and I'll sit with Him on His throne. He'll chat with me. He might show me something He'll want me to pray about. He might show me something that's going to happen and how He feels about that. He might give me a word for somebody. But sometimes He won't say anything. He just wants me to sit with Him. I don't mind those times. I simply love being with Him.

The Sound of the hooves

One time He called me up and I was standing in the throne room of God. I could see the Cherubim standing round the throne. They were massive and looked very scary! They were covered with eyes and it didn't matter where you stood, there were always eyes that could see you. It was very unnerving. When their eyes blinked, it was like a wave that went over their bodies, as they closed and opened very quickly. Their feet were like hooves and when they moved the ground shook. I was overcome by the holiness of God and fell on my face, crying out, "I'm not worthy". Jesus was standing by the throne and He said to the Cherubim, "This one is mine, he is washed in the blood". He reached out his hand to me and pulled me up and we walked past the Cherubim and went to the Father's side. Ever since I had that vision I occasionally hear the hooves of the Cherubim, shaking the ground. This reminds me of the holiness of God and how I am only worthy to enter God's presence through the blood of Jesus.

The Anchor

I was standing before the throne of God and either side were the Cherubim. In the centre of the throne there was a huge anchor, embedded into the throne. I could see a strong, thick chain attached to the anchor and it was lying along the ground in my direction. That was when I noticed that I was wearing an iron belt around my waist, firmly held together with a big lock. This was tightly closed. The other end of the chain from the anchor was attached to the belt. I looked over to the side of the throne and saw Jesus. He had a huge smile on His face and was holding a key in His hand. It was the key to the lock for my belt. I knew He held the key and was never going to unlock it and let me go. And I could never free myself from the belt. I had a hope that was anchored to the very throne of God (see Hebrews 6:9)

The Rooms of Heaven

I was in heaven and an angel began to show me round some of the rooms that were there. The first room he showed me was "The Provision Room". In this room was an incredible amount of gold coins and expensive jewellery. It was crammed everywhere. The room didn't have a floor that you could see, there were so many gold coins and jewels strewn all over it. I could see that God's monetary provision was quite literally limitless.

The next room was "The Destiny Room". Inside this room were lots and lots of scrolls, each in little drawers with people's names on. Each of these scrolls were the written out destinies from God for the individual whose name was on the drawer. It was like a library. You could open the draw for the person, pull out the scroll and read their destiny.

The next room was "The Healing Room". In the middle of this room was a big bath which was full of fragrant smelling oil. As you lay in the bath you could look up at the ceiling – which was blue and moving. It was like looking up into the skies with clouds rolling across and billowing. On the side of the bath there were new body parts which you could take and give to people who needed them. There was also a giant ladle with which you could scoop up the oil and pour onto people who couldn't make it to the bath.

The next room was a music room. I could see that there were many of these and each one represented a different style of music. The room I opened had a thumping bass sound coming out of the door. I jumped inside and started bouncing around with those people who were already there, worshipping and praising God.

I was also shown a room of restoration. This room was small, almost like a cupboard. There was a door to this room and on the door was a name panel. The name was of someone who was still living on Earth. The door was opened and I got to look inside. I could see lots of gifts. Each one was wrapped up and they all had a tag on them, with the name of the gift. I could also see part of a leg and in the corner of the room a destiny scroll. The Lord told me that each of these gifts were for things that the enemy had stolen from them. They had thought the loss was from the Lord, but He told me this was wrong – for the thief comes only to steal, rob and destroy, but He had come to give life – life in all its fullness (John 10:10). I could see that each of the gifts were much better than the things that had been lost. And this was why there was a body part there. For Satan had given them sickness to steal their health. But God was going to restore sevenfold that which had been stolen and destroyed (Proverbs 6:31). And He had a new destiny to speak out over this person. This was a very different destiny to the one that Satan had planned for them. God's plan would give them hope and a future (Jeremiah 29:11).

Well done, good and faithful servant

The father of one of my friends was ill with cancer. One night, the Lord woke me up in the early hours of the morning. He told me that He was calling the father home and He wanted me to see his entrance to heaven. I had a vision of heaven and saw this man walking up a path to Jesus. On either side of the path were people and angels. The people knew the man and gave him hugs and patted him on the back, cheering him up to Jesus. When he got to Jesus, I heard Jesus say, "Well done my good and faithful servant. Enter into the joy of your master". He then told him other things, which I wrote down. When I discovered that the father had actually died, that very morning, I was able to share the vision with my friend and the things I'd heard Jesus say to him. This brought great comfort to him and his family.

Show Me Your Glory

Moses said to the LORD, "You have been telling me, 'Lead these people,' but you have not let me know whom you will send with me. You have said, 'I know you by name and you have found favour with me.' If you are pleased with me, teach me your ways so I may know you and continue to find favour with you. Remember that this nation is your people." The LORD replied, "My Presence will go with you and I will give you rest." Then Moses said to him, "If your Presence does not go with us, do not send us up from here. How will anyone know that you are pleased with me and with your people unless you go with us? What else will distinguish me and your people from all the other people on the face of the earth?" And the LORD said to Moses, "I will do the very thing you have asked, because I am pleased with you and I know you by name." Then Moses said, "Now show me your glory." (Ex 33:12-18)

Moses had spent time in the presence of God and God promised that His Presence would go with Moses and Israel. But Moses wanted more. He asked God to show him His glory.

I was in a meeting and the worship was absolutely amazing. God's presence was powerfully manifest. I remembered Moses' request, so I asked God to show me His glory. I began to see and experience the glory of God. It was like this blinding light that just grew stronger and stronger. At the same time it felt like I was in a wind tunnel and the wind was getting stronger and stronger. I felt as though my very flesh was beginning to be blown off me. I wanted to see and experience more and more of God's glory, but I knew I couldn't do that in my present body. My desire was so strong, that I actually asked the Lord to call me home right then, so I could see His glory in all it's fullness. But God responded, "Not yet, son, not yet. There's still work for you to do". And then the experience ended. At the time the song, "Show me your glory" by Jesus Culture was playing. Now, whenever I hear that song I'm transported back to that moment and I want to see more of His glory.

Eldership Appointment

I was struggling with the appointment of an elder in our Church. We're quite conservative and this person was also conservative. I was out praying one time and complaining to God about this, asking if we could have someone different please. God called me up to heaven and invited me to sit with Him on His throne. As I sat there, I heard the voice of the person I was complaining about. He was praying for our Church, pouring out his heart to God. As I heard him pray and heard his heart, I wept. I said sorry to God for my wrong attitude about him. Too often I look at the outward appearance of someone and judge them accordingly. But God looks at their heart (1 Samuel 16:7). Ever since then I've never had a problem with that person. He did get appointed and our Church has been the better for him.

Chapter 10: The Father's Embrace

My Dad was a good man, but he was quite old-fashioned. He would never outwardly show me affection. The best he could do was to give me a handshake. My Dad died in 2010 of a heart attack. I still miss him. I had many chances to share my faith with him, but he continued to reject Christianity. The same faith that assures me that when I die I will go to be with Jesus, also tells me that I will never see my Dad again.

I was out walking one day and chatting with the Lord. I was talking about my Dad and how I would never get to experience the hug of a father, because he was no longer around. God told me that He wanted to give me a hug. He would give me the hug of a father. I stood still and could see His eyes in front of me. They were so deep and strong, they were limitless and full of love. Then He put His arms around me and pulled me in close so I could lean on His shoulder. I felt such love and warmth and I just sobbed in His arms. I stood there for quite a while. It felt like He was squeezing something out of me at the same time as filling an empty hole in my heart with His love. He told me I was His son and that He loved me deeply. I was enveloped in His love.

Ever since then I'll go out each morning for a walk and to have my father hug. I start each day with the Father's embrace and He reminds me that I'm His son and that He loves me.

Chapter 11: Dreams

Quite often I will have dreams about people. I have learnt over the years that God is doing this in order for me to pray for those people. I will wake up in the night after I've dreamt about that person and will get up and pray for them. Sometimes I will find out afterwards that something important was happening to them and the prayers were timely. I have had times where I've dreamt about something and the next day what I have dreamed will actually happen! One time I dreamt I was at a friend's house, standing in their hallway. I was apologising to them for something I had done. When I woke up I realised I needed to go and see this person and apologise. I'd never been to his house before. After I'd visited him I went to the door to leave. As I stood there with my friend in his hallway it was exactly as I'd seen it in the dream. I knew I had to say sorry to him for the thing I'd done wrong, which I did. That restored a friendship that I hadn't realised was broken.

Daniel talks about dreams as being "visions of his head as he lay in bed" (Daniel 7:1). God can speak to us through our dreams. There are lots of times recorded in the Bible where God spoke to people through their dreams. Numbers 12:6 says "When a prophet of the Lord is among you, I speak to him in visions, I speak to him in dreams". Often the language of dreams can be quite difficult to understand. But as both Daniel and Joseph said, interpretations come from God (Genesis 40:8; Daniel 2:28).

I had thought that the only way that God would speak to me in dreams was in the more literal ways that I've already mentioned. That He wouldn't speak to me through a more metaphorical dream. Then one night I had the following dream: I was standing on my own in a field and I looked up and saw a big, hot air balloon in the sky. There was a motif on it and some writing. I thought it was some sort of advertising. It was coming towards me. As it got nearer I could see that there were people inside it. I flew up to the basket and got inside it with the others. They were all chatting together about the amazing view and what they could see on the Earth. They included me in the chatting because I was also in the basket. Every now and then I would see something interesting on the Earth from the balloon and would fly out from the basket and fly over the part of the Earth I had seen. Then I would go back to the basket and chat with the others about what I'd seen. As I flew up to the balloon I could clearly see the motif and the text. The motif was a big single eye and the text said "seers".

When I woke up I thought I'd do some research on the internet and see if I could find the eye motif I'd seen. I did find it – it was called the Eye of Horus. In the Wikipedia article there was a section titled "Mathematics" which caught my attention. It turns out that the dimensions of the eye go up in powers of 2. That probably doesn't mean anything to most of you, but to me that means "binary". I'm a geek at heart, and own a binary watch. When I realised that God was speaking to me in "geek" through my dreams it made me smile. Now I take note of all my dreams and ask Him for the interpretations.

Chapter 12: Today

A couple of years ago Angela Kemm joined our Church. Hoorah! It was, coincidently, about this time that the angel of our Church changed too. He stretched his arms outwards and upwards in adoration. Then he became all fire! Every time I'm at Church and see him burning away, I'm encouraged. I believe God is going to do great things amongst us and I'm excited to see what they are. I'm still looking to grow in the prophetic and seeing. And in evangelism and seeing. And in healing and seeing. To God be all the glory!

Some of you who've read this book will have thought, "I think I'm a seer". If that's you then I'd encourage you to read the books I've listed in the recommended reading section. I'd also encourage you to step up and move in your gift. The body of Christ needs you! Find people you can trust and share your experiences with them. My prayer is that as each of plays our part, the body of Christ may be built up (Ephesians 4:12).

Recommended Reading

The School of the Seers by Jonathan Welton

Open My Eyes, Lord by Gary Oates

The Kiss of the Father by Julian C Adams

The Panoramic Seer by James Maloney

The Dancing Hand of God by James Maloney

Experiencing The Heavenly Realm by Judy Franklin & Beni Johnson

#0168 - 290517 - C0 - 210/148/4 - PB - DID1851878